Young Reed A-Z of
Sharks and Rays

Nigel Marsh

Contents

Introduction

Sharks are one of the most feared creatures on the planet, but they are also one of the most misunderstood. These majestic predators, along with their close cousins, the rays, are crucial members of a healthy and balanced marine ecosystem. Without them, our oceans would be full of sick and weak fish. While many people think that all sharks are dangerous, in reality only a handful of species have a history of biting or attacking humans. The vast majority of shark species are shy, small and harmless. In fact, humans kill millions of sharks each year, so many that some shark species are now threatened with extinction. This book is a wonderful introduction to sharks and rays. Looking at typical species and families, their biology and behavior, you'll see just how amazing these animals really are. So happy reading and have fun sorting through the A–Z of sharks and rays.

Did you know that sharks and rays belong to a class of fish known as the Chondrichthyes? But to confuse matters, they form a subclass known as Elasmobranchii. Normal fish are in a class called Osteichthyes, as they have bones, while sharks and rays are in a seperate class because they have a skeleton made of cartilage.

Did you know that scientists group sharks and rays into family groups (such as the wobbegongs or whalers) that contain species with similar physical characteristics? This may be based on body shape, fin numbers, teeth or many other physical features.

 Angel sharks

Angel sharks are bizarre flat body sharks that look like they have been squashed by a steamroller. These unusual sharks spend most of their lives hidden under a layer of sand and could be mistaken for a ray, except that angel sharks, unlike rays, have a set of very sharp teeth. There are 23 species of angel shark and they all have sandy patterned skin, this helps them to camouflage themselves on or under the sea floor. Angel sharks feed on fish, octopus and crustaceans, and being ambush predators; they wait for prey to come within striking distance before launching from the sand in a sudden attack.

A is for Angel sharks (Australian Angel Shark)

Did you know that many sharks and rays have similar body shapes, however rays always have their gills on the underside of their body? Shark gills on the other hand are located on the top or side of their body.

A is for Associates of sharks
(Lemon Shark covered in Suckerfish)

Associates of sharks

Many shark species travel in schools, but others like to keep their own company. Despite this, sharks are never truly alone as a number of fish species live in close company with these predators. The most common of these associates are the suckerfish or remoras. Suckerfish have suction pads on their heads that allow them to attach themselves to sharks and rays. There are many benefits from this association for the suckerfish, such as enjoying a free ride and sharing the food of their host. Other small fish, such as pilot fish and juvenile trevally, like to stick close to sharks as they get protection from larger fish that would otherwise eat them.

Did you know that some fish, like trevally and cobia, rub themselves against sharks to remove lose scales and parasites, much to the annoyance of the shark?

7

B Blind shark

The blind shark is found only off the east coast of Australia and spends most of the day hiding under ledges to avoid being eaten by larger sharks. Blind sharks grow to 1.2m (4ft) in length and acquired their unusual name not because they are blind, but because the first fishermen to capture this species found they close their eyes when taken out of water. Like a lot of other small sharks, blind sharks are nocturnal and feed on small prey like crabs, shrimps and cuttlefish.

B is for Blind shark (Blind Shark)

Did you know that the first sharks evolved around 450 million years ago? Most of the sharks that we see today have been around for 100 million years, meaning that sharks were around when dinosaurs ruled the earth.

B is for Black-tip Reef Shark (Black-tip Reef Shark)

Did you know that only about ten people are killed by sharks each year? Many more are killed by dogs, bees, falling coconuts, ants, mosquitoes and even cows.

Black-tip reef shark

One of the most common shark species found on coral reefs in the Pacific and Indian Oceans is the black-tip reef shark. Although common, this species is shy and spends a lot of time in very shallow water, often less than a metre (3ft) deep. A member of the large whaler family, black-tip reef sharks grow to 1.8m (6ft) long and are generally considered harmless. Snorkelers encounter black-tip reef sharks on shallow reef flats where the sharks hunt for their preferred prey of fish and octopus.

C Catsharks

Catsharks look nothing like a cat, but got their name due to their cat-like eyes that reflect light at night. This large family of sharks contains over 100 species. They inhabit all the oceans of the world, from shallow to very deep water. Catsharks are usually quite small; most are less than 1m (3ft) long. Catsharks also lay eggs, which attach to seaweeds and corals. Most catsharks are rarely seen during the day, as they hide in caves or under seaweed, but emerge at night to feed on a variety of fish, crustaceans and molluscs.

Did you know that some catshark species are called swell sharks, as they swallow water? The water expands their stomach to make them appear larger as a way to frighten off potential predators.

C is for Catsharks (Draughtboard Shark)

C is for Caribbean Reef Shark

Did you know that there are actually more species of rays than sharks? There are around 560 ray species identified.

Caribbean reef shark

The Caribbean reef shark is found in the Western Atlantic Ocean and it is the most common species found on coral reefs in this area. Reaching a length of 3m (10ft), the Caribbean reef shark is considered dangerous and has been responsible for a number of attacks on humans. A member of the large whaler family, the Caribbean reef shark is a common visitor to shark feeds in the Caribbean, with thousands of divers enjoying a close encounter with this species each year.

D Diving with sharks

Many people have an intense fear of sharks and would do anything to avoid encountering one, but divers go out of their way to see these amazing creatures underwater. Most sharks and rays are harmless to divers. They are also generally shy, so encounters with these creatures are more rare than most people would think. In Australia, bottom dwelling sharks like wobbegongs and Port Jackson sharks are the most commonly encountered, as they spend most of the day sleeping and are easy to approach. Reef sharks and other free swimming sharks are harder to approach and generally keep their distance from bubble blowing divers. Of course, to see the most famous shark of them all, the great white shark, the safety of a shark cage is the best way to go.

D is for Diving with sharks (Spotted Wobbegong Shark)

Did you know that shark diving tours are very popular, with divers travelling around the world and spending thousands of dollars just to encounter sharks in their natural habitat?

Dangerous bull shark

The bull shark belongs to a very unique group of marine animals that can live in both fresh water and salt water. While a number of other shark and ray species can also do this, the bull shark is the best adapted to this transition and have even been found 4000km (2485 miles) from the ocean, in the Amazon River. The bull shark is a member of the whaler family and is found in tropical waters around the world. They grow to 3.5m (11.5ft) in length and obtained their common name from their stocky shape. With a varied diet that includes fish, turtles and other sharks, bull sharks are opportunistic feeders that will bite almost anything, including people swimming in murky water. This has given them a reputation as one of the world's most dangerous sharks.

D is for Dangerous Bull Shark (Bull Shark)

Did you know that some sharks have been found to be as intelligent as mammals, and they can even be trained? At Shark Reef in Fiji, wild bull sharks have been trained to be hand fed by divers, and will only get food if they follow a set of strict rules.

E Eagle rays

Eagle rays are one of the few families of rays that spend most of their time swimming in mid-water, soaring like an eagle. 23 species of eagle rays have been identified living in shallow tropical and temperate waters. These rays have long tails, usually a few tail spines and well-pronounced heads, with either a rounded or pointed snout. Eagle rays are strong, graceful swimmers and are sometimes found in large schools. They feed on small fish, worms, molluscs and crustaceans, most of which they dig out of the sand with their snouts.

E is for Eagle rays (Spotted Eagle Ray)

Did you know that eagle rays are often seen jumping clear of the water? It is not known why they do this, but it may be to dislodge parasites, to escape predators or maybe just for fun.

Did you know that marine leeches like to attach to sharks and rays and feed off their blood?

Electric rays

Most people will never encounter an electric ray, but those that have will never forget the experience, as it can be quite shocking! These unusual rays have developed modified muscles that can generate electric shocks, which they use for defence and hunting. There are several families of electric rays and around 70 species. The amount of voltage they can produce will depend on their size, with the largest rays producing zaps of 200 volts. This is enough to numb your hand and to teach you to never touch one of these small chubby rays again.

E is for Electric rays (Short-tailed Electric Ray)

F Fiddler rays

Three species of fiddler rays are found in the waters of southern Australia. These distinctive rays have the body of a shark and a round flat head that is shaped like a fiddle or banjo. These rays are members of a family called the shovelnose rays, as all have a shovel-shaped head. Fiddler rays are harmless. They possess no tail barbs, and only have small blunt teeth to feed on fish, molluscs and crustaceans. During the day they either bury themselves under the sand or hide under kelp, coming out at night to hunt for food.

F is for Fiddler Rays
(Eastern Fiddler Ray)

Did you know that new species of sharks and rays are still being discovered each year? Many are from deep water, but there are still many shallow reef species awaiting discovery.

F is for Fin walkers (Milne Bay Epaulette Shark)

Fin walkers (epaulette sharks)

Epaulette sharks are long, slender bodied sharks that live on shallow tropical reefs. These small sharks are part of the long-tail carpet shark family, which includes 16 species that are rarely more than 1m (3ft) long. Epaulette sharks are also known as walking sharks, as they use their fins to slowly walk across the bottom while looking for food or a place to shelter. During the day these harmless sharks like to wedge themselves in caves or under coral, only to emerge at night to feed on crustaceans, small fish and worms.

Did you know that sharks never need dental work as they possess several rows of teeth? Each time one gets broken another one quickly replaces the missing tooth.

G Grey reef shark

Grey reef sharks are occasionally territorial and have bitten a small number of divers that have encroached on their territory. This species grows to 1.8m (6ft) in length and is found in tropical waters throughout the Indo-Pacific region. A member of the whaler family, which contains around 50 species, grey reef sharks are often found in large groups, especially on current-swept reefs. Grey reef sharks generally pose little threat to people, but if they drop their fins and start swimming by twisting their bodies, it is a message to back off, as you have encroached on their territory.

G is for Grey Reef Shark (Grey Reef Shark)

Did you know that most large shark species have to continuously keep swimming to survive? If they stop swimming they cannot push water through their gills and drown.

G is for Grey Nurse Shark (Grey Nurse Shark)

Grey nurse shark

The grey nurse shark reaches a length of 3.2m (10ft 5in) and belongs to a small family of sharks known as the sandtiger sharks. Four species of shark are found in this family that live in temperate to subtropical waters throughout the world. These sharks have fearsome looking teeth that project out of the mouth. However, these sharks are considered harmless, with these dagger-like teeth designed to catch fish, rays and small sharks. For many decades the fearsome look of the grey nurse shark caused it to be tagged a 'man-eater', even though this species is quite docile and has never killed a human. This fear led to the grey nurse shark almost being wiped out in Australia. Today the grey nurse shark is listed as critically endangered.

Did you know that the grey nurse shark was the first shark in the world to be protected? Laws were passed in Australia in 1984 to stop this species being killed.

19

H Hammerhead sharks

With their bizarre wing-shaped heads, hammerhead sharks are one of the most unique looking animals in the world. Hammerheads are thought to be one of the most recently evolved sharks. Their wide head enhances their sense of sight, smell and their prey-detecting abilities by spreading them over a wider area. There are 11 species of hammerhead sharks found worldwide which range in size from the 1m (3ft) long bonnethead shark to the 6m (19ft) long great hammerhead shark. Each species seems to feed on different prey. Larger members of the family feed on sharks, large fish and rays, while smaller species feed on crustaceans, small fish and molluscs.

H is for Hammerhead sharks (Great Hammerhead Shark)

Did you know that great hammerheads love to eat stingrays? Even though they get jabbed by stingray tail spines, and some have been recorded with over 50 spines stuck in their head.

Did you know that there are 13 ray families and all of them give birth to live young, except the skates, who lay eggs called mermaids purses?

Horn sharks

Horn sharks are easily distinguished from other sharks as they have spines in front of their dorsal fins and ridges over the eyes. Nine species have been identified from around the world and all are docile and harmless. Horn sharks have blunt plate-like teeth, which they use to break up the shells of prey, such as molluscs and crustaceans. These sharks lay unusual spiral shaped egg cases, which are often found washed up on beaches after a storm. The largest horn shark is the Port Jackson shark, which is only found in the waters around southern Australia and reaches a length of 1.7m (5ft).

H is for Horn sharks (Port Jackson Shark)

I Inert white-tip reef shark

Numerous shark species inhabit coral reefs, but the most common is the white-tip reef shark, seen in the Indian and Pacific Oceans. Another member of the large whaler family, the white-tip reef shark grows to a length of 2.1m (7ft) and is most often found resting on the sea floor during the day. They are one of the few large shark species that can stop swimming and remain inert on the sea floor, as they have learnt to suck in water to breath. At night they are far more active, hunting on the reef and feeding on sleeping fish.

I is for Inert White-tip Reef shark (White-tip Reef Shark)

Did you know that most shark species are cold blooded, like fish, but a handful of species, like the great white and mako are warm blooded?

J is for Jaws (Great White Shark)

Did you know that some shark species swim great distances? A tagged great white shark was found to swim from South Africa to Australia and back, all in nine months.

J Jaws (great white shark)

The movie 'Jaws' turned an already notorious creature, the great white shark, into public enemy number one. This large shark is the most feared predator on the planet and is responsible for stopping many people from entering the water, even in areas where it is not found. This master predator reaches a length of 6.5m (21ft) and feeds on sharks, rays, dolphins, seals and turtles. The great white shark is found in temperate to subtropical waters around the globe. These sharks have attacked quite a number of swimmers, surfers and divers. Most attacks are considered a case of mistaken identity with the shark confusing the person for its normal prey. Although dangerous, the great white shark is an important member of the food chain and is quickly becoming endangered due to fishing pressures.

K Kite-like skates

Skates are kite-shaped rays that live mostly in very deep water. This large family of rays contains over 200 members. Most are small, less than a metre wide, but a few of the larger members of the family reach widths of over 2m (6ft). Skates are one of the few ray species that don't have tail spines, but many instead have sharp thorns covering their tails and back. Skates feed by digging in the sand and mud, and preying on molluscs, crustaceans and small fish.

K is for Kite-like skates (Melbourne Skate)

Did you know that there are 509 species of shark so far discovered, but of these only a dozen species are considered dangerous? Most sharks are completely harmless.

L Lemon sharks

Like many other shark species, lemon sharks look nothing like their namesakes. However, these sharks sometimes have yellow skin, which explains the odd name. The two lemon shark species are members of the whaler family and live on tropical coral reefs. They reach 3.4m (11ft) in length and are generally considered a non-aggressive species. Surprisingly, some lemon sharks enjoy the company of divers and allow people to pat them. Lemon sharks are often found in very shallow water and the females are known to enter mangroves to give birth to their young. The young lemon sharks remain in the mangroves until they are big enough to head into deeper water and avoid being eaten by larger sharks.

L is for Lemon sharks (Lemon Shark

Did you know that sharks come in such a wide variety of shapes and sizes that they are split into 34 family groups of similar species?

M Manta rays

Manta rays are a member of the devil ray family, so named as they have fins on each side of their head that can be rolled up to resemble horns. Far from being devil-like, manta rays are very playful and as such they are the most sought after ray for snorkelers and divers to swim with. Two species of manta ray are found in tropical and subtropical waters. The biggest is the oceanic manta ray that reaches a massive 7m (22ft) wide, but the small reef manta ray isn't exactly tiny, reaching a width of 5.5m (18ft). These giant rays feed on tiny shrimps and other creatures known as plankton, which are collected by their very wide mouth.

M is for Manta rays (Reef Manta Ray)

Did you know that manta rays, and many other shark and ray species visit cleaning stations each day to get parasites removed? Groups of tiny cleaner wrasse provide an invaluable service removing unwanted bugs from the bodies of sharks and rays.

Mako sharks

Considered to be the fastest of all the sharks, mako sharks chase and capture powerful billfish. Quite a few have been recorded with bills embedded in their body. Two species of mako sharks have been identified, the short-fin mako and the very rare long-fin mako. Both species grow to 3.9m (12ft) in length and are a bluish shade, which makes them difficult to see underwater. Mako sharks are considered dangerous, but are generally wary of divers, posing more of a threat to spearfishermen. Mako sharks are found around the world in both tropical and temperate waters.

Did you know that most sharks swim at a speed of around 8km (5 miles) per hour, but can reach speeds of 19km (12 miles) per hour when chasing prey? The fastest shark in the ocean, the short-fin mako, can reach speeds of 50km (31 miles) per hour.

M is for Mako sharks (Short-fin Mako Shark)

N Nurse sharks

Three species of nurse sharks inhabit the tropical waters of the world. They are one of the largest sharks encountered on coral reefs as they grow to 3.2m (10ft) long. However, they are quite harmless with only a small set of teeth and spend most of their day sleeping, usually hidden away in caves. These sharks feed on fish, octopus and crabs and use a sucking action to grab prey. This sucking noise is said to sound like a baby being nursed, and may be the reason for the usual name of this family of sharks.

N is for Nurse sharks (Tawny Nurse Shark)

Did you know that sharks and rays have skin that is covered in small teeth, and it is so rough that it was once used as sandpaper?

O Ocean giant (whale shark)

The only member of the whale shark family is a rather unforgettable gentle giant of the oceans. This huge shark, which grows to 14m (46ft) in length, has a broad flat head, a very wide mouth and skin decorated with rows of spots and stripes. For all their immense size whale sharks have small teeth and feed on plankton, a soup of tiny shrimps and other small critters. Whale sharks are found in tropical waters around the globe, and swimming with these amazing ocean giants is a very popular tourist attraction.

Did you know that the whale shark is one of the longest living of all the sharks and it is estimated that they live around 100 years?

O is for Ocean giant (Whale Shark)

P Primitive cow sharks

Cow sharks are considered to be one of the most primitive of all the sharks, unchanged for millions of years. This family of sharks, which contains 37 species, is mainly found in deep water, but a few species do venture into shallow bays. The broadnose sevengill shark is probably the best known member of the cow shark family. Divers occasionally encounter this species in shallow temperate waters. Cow sharks vary in size from 1.4m (5ft) to 5.5m (17ft) and feed on a varied diet of fish, crustaceans, other sharks and even seals.

P is for Primitive Cow sharks (Broadnose Sevengill Shark)

Did you know that almost all sharks and rays have five paired gill slits, apart from the cow sharks which have either six or seven gills?

Q is for Quirky Porcupine Ray (Porcupine Ray)

Q Quirky Porcupine Ray

One of the most quirky and unusual members of the stingray family would have to be the porcupine ray. This rather large ray grows to 1.5m (4.9ft) in width and unlike other stingray species it doesn't have a tail spine. Instead. the porcupine ray is covered in sharp thorns, hence the unusual name. The porcupine ray is thought to have developed tough thorny skin as a defence against great hammerhead sharks, which like to eat stingrays. But its tough skin hasn't defended it against humans, with many Asian cultures capturing this species just for its skin. The Japanese Samurai used this thorny skin for sword grips, while the Malays used it to cover their shields. The porcupine ray is found throughout the Indo-Pacific region, but is considered a rare species.

Did you know that sharks have very good eye sight and can see twice as effective as cats at night?

R Reproduction

Sharks and rays reproduce by either laying eggs or giving birth to live young. Unlike fish they don't spawn and release millions of eggs, but instead produce a smaller number of well-formed young, much like mammals do. Sex between sharks is often very difficult, as they don't have hands, so the male has to bite the female to hold on to her. The pregnancy period and the number of young produced varies greatly between species. Some species have huge litters of close to one hundred young like the tiger shark, while others only produce one or two young like the grey nurse shark.

R is for Reproduction (Above: Ornate Wobbegong Sharks courting) and (Left: Draughtboard Shark egg case)

Did you know that some female sharks have skin that is twice as thick as the male? This is to prevent injury while mating.

Round stingrays

The smallest members of the ray family are called stingarees, but they are also commonly known as round stingrays. Stingarees are easily identified from stingrays by their small size, generally around 30cm (12in) wide, their round shape and short tails. Around 40 species of stingarees are known and most of these have been recorded in the waters around Australia. Stingarees find their food by digging in the sand and eat worms, crustaceans and molluscs. All stingarees have tail spines to defend themselves against sharks. A number of people get jabbed by them each year, especially when wading in shallow water.

R is for Round stingrays (Kapala Stingaree)

Did you know that when sharks are rolled on their back, they go into a form of sleep called tonic immobility? Shark researchers use this technique to safely handle large sharks while tagging or taking blood samples.

S Shovelnose rays

Shovelnose rays have got a very distinctive nose and head that looks very similar to a shovel. But they don't really use it like a shovel to dig up prey. Instead the 40 members of this family of rays dig in the sand with their mouth to find their preferred food of shrimps, small fish, shellfish and worms. These unusual looking rays have a ray-like head, but the rest of their body is similar to a shark, leading to a lot of people mistakenly calling them shovelnose sharks.

S is for Shovelnose rays (Eastern Shovelnose Ray)

Did you know that the smallest shark so far discovered is the dwarf lantern shark and it only grows to a length of 18cm (7in).

S is for Stingrays (Cowtail Stingray and Pink Stingray)

Did you know that the most common fossil found around the world are sharks teeth?

Stingrays

Stingrays are one of the better known ray families, because most live in shallow water and are regularly encountered by snorkelers and divers. Around 60 species of stingrays have been identified in tropical and temperate waters. All stingrays are potentially dangerous, as they have sharp spines on their tails. These dagger-like spines are used for defence against sharks, but a number of humans have also been stabbed accidently after stepping on or cornering a stingray. Most stingrays inhabit shallow reefs, bays and estuaries, but a few live in rivers, including the giant freshwater stingray that grows to 2m (7ft) wide.

T Thresher sharks

With a tail longer than their body, thresher sharks are one of the more unusual members of the shark family. Three species of thresher sharks are found in the temperate and tropical oceans of the world, which vary in size from 3m (10ft) to 6m (20ft), which includes their very long tails. These sharks are quite rare and live most of their lives in deep ocean waters. They have large eyes, to help them see in the dark waters where they live and a small mouth. They feed on a variety of small schooling fish and squid. Divers rarely encounter thresher sharks, except on the top of underwater mountains, where these sharks are known to visit to get serviced by cleaner fish.

T is for Thresher sharks (Pelagic Thresher Shark)

Did you know that thresher sharks evolved their very long tails to catch fish? They crack their tails over their heads just like a whip to stun their prey.

Did you know that sharks and rays don't have a single bone in their bodies? Their skeletons are made entirely on cartilage, just like the human nose.

Tiger shark

The tiger shark is the largest and potentially most dangerous member of the whaler shark family. This shark grows to almost 6m (20ft) in length and is easily identified by its rounded snout and the dark vertical bars along its body. Tiger sharks are found in tropical to warm temperate water around the world. These sharks feed on almost anything they can catch – turtles, fish, rays, sharks, crustaceans, sea snakes, sea birds, molluscs and marine mammals. They are the ultimate ocean cleaners and their stomachs have been found to contain all sorts of rubbish, even car number plates. Tiger sharks have attacked and killed swimmers, surfers and divers, and they should always be treated with respect.

U Under threat

Until recently, very few shark species were killed for food. Most were killed for sport or to make beaches safer. But over the last thirty years millions upon millions of sharks have been killed for their fins to make shark fin soup. Considered a delicacy in Asian countries, the demand for shark fin soup sees around 100 million sharks of all species killed each year. This slaughter has led to a massive drop in shark numbers worldwide and many species have declined by 90 per cent or more. Shark finning has been banned in many countries, but until it is banned everywhere many shark species will continue to face the threat of extinction.

U is for Under threat (Great White Shark)

Did you know that it is not safe to eat most shark species as their flesh often contains high levels of mercury, which is very dangerous to your health?

V is for Varied Catshark (Varied Catshark)

Did you know that the largest shark to
ever live was the now extinct megalodon,
a close relative of the great white shark?
This giant shark grew to 18m (59ft) in
length and had teeth that were 17cm
(7in) long.

V Varied catshark

The varied catshark is also known as the necklace catshark as it looks like it is wearing
a pretty spotted necklace. This little shark reaches a maximum length of 90cm (35in)
and is only found in the cool waters of southern Australia. A member of the collared
catshark family, which only contains four members, the varied catshark feeds on small
fish and crabs. This shark species spends most hours of the day sleeping under seaweed,
sometimes in water only a metre deep.

W Wobbegongs

The name wobbegong comes from the Australian Aboriginal word meaning 'shaggy beard' which is a great description of the unusual fleshy frills around the heads of these bizarre-looking sharks. Wobbegongs use these beards, and their bright skin patterns, to blend in with the sea floor. They are ambush predators and wait many hours for prey to swim close enough to be grabbed. The 12 species of wobbegongs have very sharp teeth and eat fish, octopus, rays and even other sharks. Wobbegongs vary in length from 1m (3ft) to 3m (10ft), and are generally considered harmless unless harassed by people touching them.

W is for Wobbegongs (Banded Wobbegong Shark)

Did you know that the wobbegong is also known as the carpet shark, as their skin patterns look like a very ornate carpet?

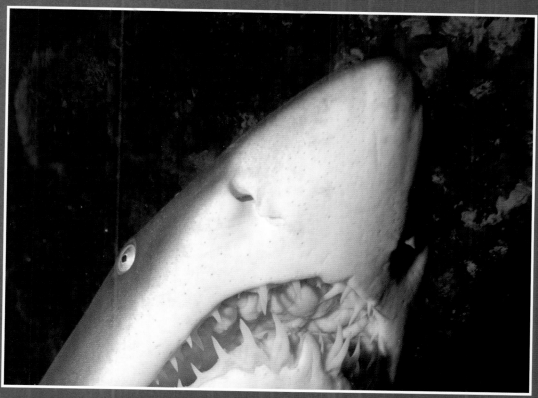

X is for X-ray senses (the Ampullae of Lorenizi on the nose of the Grey Nurse Shark)

X   X-ray senses

Sharks and rays have all the regular senses that animals have – sight, hearing, touch, taste and smell. But they also have a few extra ones that give them very special abilities. The first of these additional senses is their lateral line, a unique sense that all fish have, that allows sharks and rays to detect vibrations and movement in the water around them. This lateral line runs down the length of their body and consists of tiny hair cells that are extremely sensitive. Another special sense that sharks and rays have evolved is the ability to detect electrical fields generated by another living animal. Sharks and rays have thousands of tiny canals on their heads called the *Ampullae of Lorenzini* that detects these electrical fields. Sharks and rays use all their senses when searching for prey and also to avoid becoming prey themselves.

Did you know that sharks and rays might be able to detect magnetic fields, which they may possibly use to navigate the oceans of the world?

Young sharks and rays

Shark and rays have no parental attachment to their young and once the young, called pups, are born or hatched they have to fend for themselves. Young sharks and rays look like miniature versions of their parents, however they are rarely seen as they end up being eaten by their older cousins. To avoid being eaten, young sharks and rays hide in caves, under ledges, in mangroves, under sand, in estuaries or in deep water. To give the young the best chance of survival they at least give birth to rather large young that are ready to feed and fight as soon as they emerge.

Y is for Young sharks and rays (young Port Jackson Shark)

Did you know that grey nurse shark embryos eat each other in the uterus, with only the strongest pup in each uterus surviving?

Z is for Zebra Shark (Zebra Shark)

Did you know that many shark species migrate with the changing seasons? Some move up and down the coast following preferred water temperatures, while others move from shallow to deep water. But many of these migrations are still a complete mystery.

Z Zebra shark

The zebra shark could be called the most beautifully patterned shark of all. Identified by their leopard-like skin pattern, these large sharks, reaching 2.5m (8ft) in length, are found in the tropical waters of the Indian and Pacific Oceans. They are known as the zebra shark because the young have zebra-like stripes. However, as the young are rarely seen, many people also call them leopard sharks. Zebra sharks feed on crustaceans and molluscs, and have tiny teeth designed to crush the shells of their prey. A popular shark with divers, zebra sharks are easy to approach and spent much of the day resting on the sea floor.

Quiz time

Once you have read the book you can test your newfound
knowledge of sharks and rays by taking this quick quiz.

1. What shark species is the largest?
2. What is the most common fossil on earth?
3. How many shark species are there?
4. What is the major threat to most shark species?
5. What shark looks like a carpet?
6. Do sharks have any bones?
7. Which shark can live in both salt water and fresh water?
8. Which rays have a shovel shaped head?
9. Do Port Jackson sharks lay eggs?
10. Why shouldn't you ever touch an electric ray?

For quiz answers go to page 47.

Photography

The author, Nigel Marsh, who has been diving with sharks and rays for almost forty years, took most of the photographs appearing in this book. The author would like to thank the other talented photographers that provided images, Mary Malloy (great white shark and Melbourne skate) and Brandon Cole (short-fin mako shark and broadnose sevengill shark) to illustrate this book.

Smooth Stingray

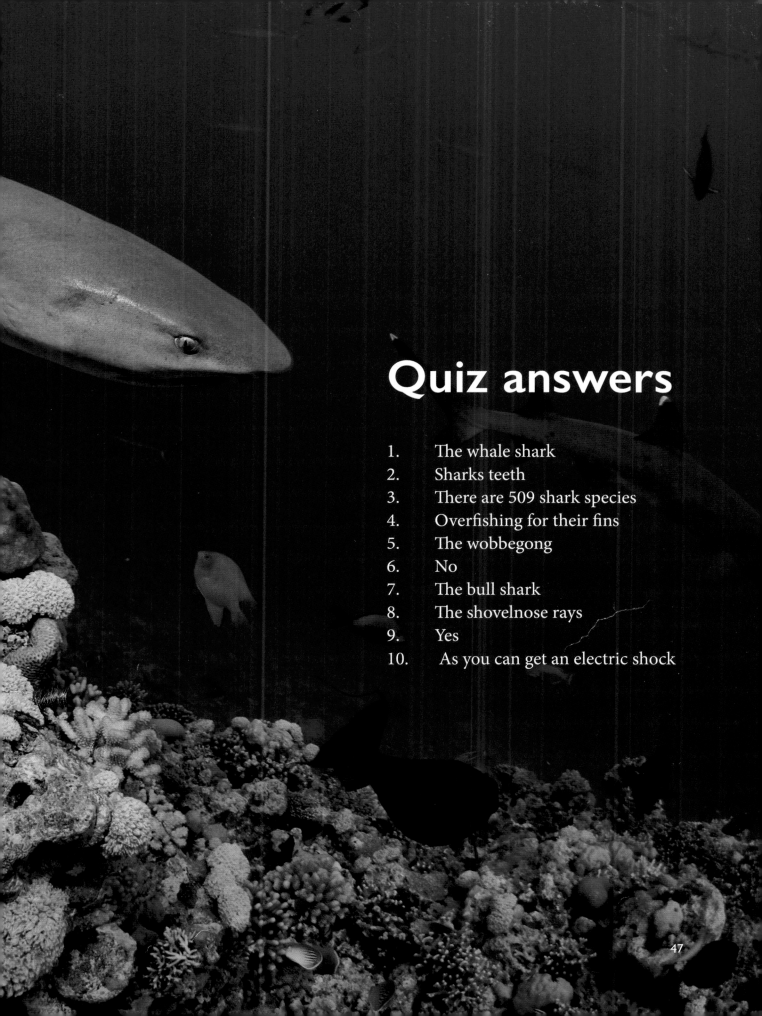

Quiz answers

1. The whale shark
2. Sharks teeth
3. There are 509 shark species
4. Overfishing for their fins
5. The wobbegong
6. No
7. The bull shark
8. The shovelnose rays
9. Yes
10. As you can get an electric shock

First published in 2016 by New Holland Publishers Pty Ltd
London • Sydney • Auckland

The Chandlery Unit 704 50 Westminster Bridge Road London SE1 7QY United Kingdom
1/66 Gibbes Street Chatswood NSW 2067 Australia
5/39 Woodside Ave Northcote, Auckland 0627 New Zealand

www.newhollandpublishers.com

A record of this book is held at the British Library and the National Library of Australia.

ISBN 9781921580307

Managing Director: Fiona Schultz
Publisher: Diane Ward
Project Editor: Jessica McNamara
Designer: Peter Guo and Andrew Davies
Production Director: Olga Dementiev
Printer: Toppan Leefung Printing Limited

10 9 8 7 6 5 4 3 2 1

Keep up with New Holland Publishers on Facebook
www.facebook.com/NewHollandPublishers

US: $14.99
UK: £9.99